Basic Tools

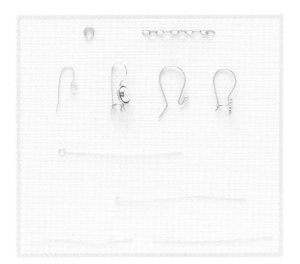

Basic Findings

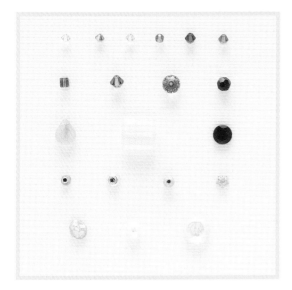

Basic Beads

Elegant
Stylish
Sparkling
Pretty

for All
Ages and
Reasons!

Do you prefer dazzling dangles or the peaceful radiance of pearls? No matter what your style, you will find irresistible earrings to make for yourself or as a gift for someone special.

Elegant Earrings to wear each day...

Elegant and Pretty

Easy and Fun to Make

for All Ages and Reasons!

You'll love making every beautiful pair!

Bouncy and Beautiful

Stylish and Sparkling

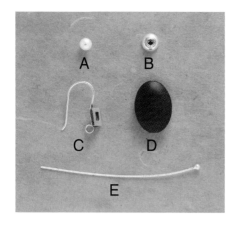

Black & Pearl Earrings

Tasteful, refined, and perfect for New Year's eve or the Governor's ball, black and silver are a winning combination when you need an extra special piece of jewelry.

Materials:
2 black 13mm x 18mm onyx beads (D)
2 white 3mm x 4mm pearls (A)
2 sterling 3" ball head pins (E)
6mm sterling bead cap (B)
pair of sterling ear wires (C)
round-nose pliers

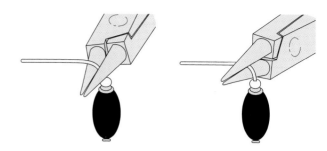

Thread a black bead, bead cap and a pearl on a head pin. Grasp the pin with pliers about 1/8" from the end of the jaws. The pliers should be touching the top of the pearl. Bend the wire at a 90° angle . Pivot the pliers from horizontal to vertical.

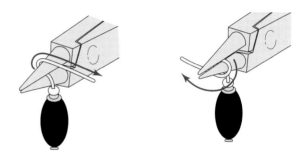

Wrap the wire around the top jaw of the pliers. Reposition wire on the bottom jaw of the pliers.

Wrap wire around the bottom jaw of the pliers.

Grasp the loop of the dangle with the pliers Without touching the pearl, begin coiling the short end around the neck of the dangle. Begin coils as close to the loop as possible. Make two or three coils, then clip the end of the wire close to the coils.

Open the loop on the ear wire and thread on the earring. Close the ear wire loop.

Repeat all steps for the remaining earring.

With pliers, form a small spiral with 3 loops at the end of a piece of wire .

Thread a crystal on the wire. Grasp wire pin with the pliers about $1/8"$ from the end of the jaws. The pliers should be touching the top of the crystal.

Bend the wire at a 90° angle . Pivot the pliers from horizontal to vertical.

Wrap the wire around the top jaw of the pliers.
Reposition wire on the bottom jaw of the pliers.
Wrap the wire around the bottom jaw of the pliers.

Slip the top link of the chain onto the loop of the dangle and grasp the loop of the dangle with the pliers. Without touching the crystal, begin coiling the short end around the neck of the dangle.

Begin the coils as close to the loop as possible. Make two or three coils, then clip the end of the wire close to the coils.

Make dangles with remaining crystals and attach to chain.

Open ear wire loop and thread chain on the earring. Close the ear wire loop.

Repeat all steps for the remaining earring.

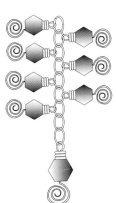

Black Crystal Spirals

Next time he puts on his tux and you slip into that stunning little black dress, catch his attention with black AB crystals that sparkle as much as your eyes.

designed by Jane Merchant

Materials:
Black AB Swarovski crystals (fourteen 6mm, two 8mm)(A)
two 1" pieces of gold filled chain with 3mm x 4mm links (C)
sixteen 5" pieces of 24 gauge gold wire (D)
pair of gold filled ear wires (B)
round-nose pliers

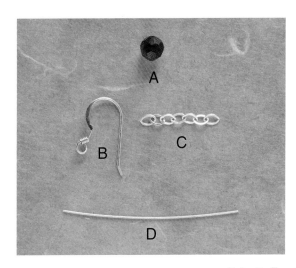

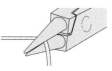

Grasp one end of a piece of wire with pliers about ¹/₈"
from the end of the jaws. Bend the wire at a 90° angle.
Pivot the pliers from horizontal to vertical.
Wrap the wire around the top jaw of the pliers.

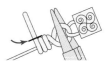

Reposition the wire on the bottom jaw of the pliers.
Wrap the wire around the bottom jaw of the pliers.
Slip the ear wire on the loop. Grasp the loop with the pliers. Begin coiling one end around the neck of the link. Begin the coils as close to the loop as possible. Make two or three coils, then clip the end of the wire close to the coils.

Slip a crystal on the wire and make a wrapped loop around the last link in a 2" piece of chain.

Make another wrapped loop around the ear wire. Thread on a crystal and make a wrapped loop around the last link of a 1¹/₂" piece of chain.

Make another wrapped loop around the ear wire. Thread on a crystal and a make a wrapped loop around the last link of a 1" piece of chain.

Thread a teardrop with a 4" piece of 24 gauge sterling silver wire. Arrange the wire so that one side is shorter than the other. Cross the ends of the wire. Then bend the ends at a 90 degree angle.

Grasp the longer wire with pliers about ¹/₈" from the end of the jaws. Bend the wire at a 90° angle.

Pivot the pliers from horizontal to vertical. Wrap the wire around the top jaw of the pliers

Reposition the wire on the bottom jaw of the pliers. Wrap the wire around the bottom jaw of the pliers.

Thread on one of the end links of the chain. Grasp the loop with the pliers. Begin coiling one end around both wires. Begin coils as close to the loop as possible. Make two or three coils, then clip the end of the coiling wire and the straight wire close to the coils.

Make dangles with remaining teardrops attached to other end of chains as shown at right.
Repeat above steps for the remaining earring.

Triple Drop

*Next time you need a soft, feminine
earring, try the misty texture and subtle
color in these chalcedony teardrops. The
tiny bicone crystals and fine sterling wire
complement the stones perfectly.*

Materials:
two 9mm x12mm top-drilled blue chalcedony
   teardrops (C)
two blue and two green top-drilled 10mm x10mm
   chalcedony teardrops (B)
Swarovski bicone crystals: four 4mm light blue,
   two 4mm light green (A)
pieces of sterling silver chain with 2mm links:
   two 2", two 1¹/₂", two 1" (E)
12 four-inch pieces of 24 gauge sterling silver wire (F)
pair of sterling silver ear wires (D)
round-nose pliers

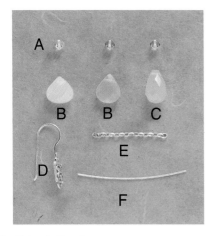

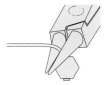 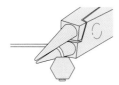

Thread a crystal on a head pin. Grasp the pin with pliers about 1/8" from the end of the jaws. The pliers should be touching the top of the crystal.

Bend the wire at a 90° angle. Pivot the pliers from horizontal to vertical.

Wrap the wire around the top jaw of the pliers.

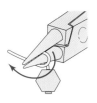 

Reposition the wire on the bottom jaw of the pliers. Wrap the wire around the bottom jaw of the pliers.

Grasp the loop of the dangle with the pliers. Without touching the crystal, begin coiling the short end around the neck of the dangle. Begin coils as close to the loop as possible. Make two or three coils, then clip the end of the wire close to the coils.

Repeat steps 1-5 for a total of 2 crystal and 3 pearl dangles.

Grasp one of the 4" pieces of wire with the pliers about 1/8" from the end of the jaws. Bend the wire at a 90° angle.

Pivot the pliers from horizontal to vertical.

Wrap the wire around the top jaw of the pliers.

Reposition the wire on the bottom jaw of the pliers. Wrap the wire around the bottom jaw of the pliers.

Slip all dangles on the loop alternating crystals and pearls. Grasp the loop with the pliers. Without touching the bead on the head pin, begin coiling the short end around the neck. Begin coils as close to the loop as possible. Make two or three coils, then clip the end of the wire close to the coils. Bend loop at a right angle and slip through the hole in the top of the blister pearl.

Make a wrapped loop at the top of the blister pearl.

Repeat all steps for the remaining earring.

Open the loops on the ear wires and thread on the earrings. Close the ear wire loops.

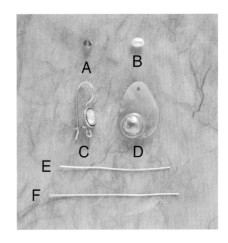

Blister Pearl

Blister pearl teardrops reflect the shimmering radiance of the cluster pearls and bicones to create a combination symbolizing both warmth and wealth.

designed by Jane Merchant

Materials:
2 green 4mm Swarovski bicones (A)
6 white 3mm x 4mm pearls (B)
10 sterling 1 1/2" flat head pins (F)
2 four-inch pieces of 22 gauge sterling wire (E)
2 12mm x 23mm blister pearl teardrops (D)
pair of sterling ear wires (C)
round-nose pliers

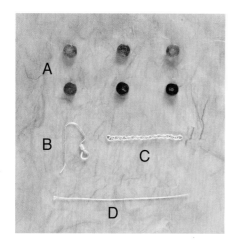

Tourmaline Drops

Natural stones make beautiful jewelry that is simply irresistible and simply made. You are going to love the results of this so-simple technique.

Materials:
3mm x 6mm tourmaline disk beads: 6 brownish green, 6 pink (A)
two 11/2" pieces of sterling silver chain with 3mm x 4mm links (C)
twelve 11/2" head pins with ball ends (D)
pair of sterling silver ear wires (B)
round-nose pliers
wire cutters

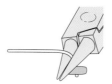 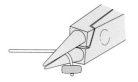

Thread a disk bead on a head pin. Grasp the pin with pliers about $1/8$" from the end of the jaws. The pliers should be touching the top of the crystal. Bend the wire at a 90° angle

Pivot the pliers from horizontal to vertical.

Wrap the wire around the top jaw of pliers. Reposition the wire on the bottom jaw of the pliers. Wrap the wire around the bottom jaw of the pliers as shown.

Slip the straight end of the head pin through the fourth link from the top of the chain and grasp the loop of the dangle with the pliers.

Without touching the disk bead begin coiling the short end around the neck of the dangle. Begin the coils as close to the loop as possible.

Make two or three coils, then clip the end of the wire close to the coils.

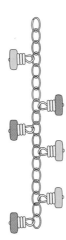

Make dangles with remaining crystals and attach to chain.

Open ear wire loop and thread chain on the earring. Close the ear wire loop.

Repeat above steps for the remaining earring.

Thread bead onto head pin, and grasp with 3-in-1 beading tool at location where base of loop is desired (our design leaves a neck in the head pin). Bend the wire over the tool's jaw to make a sharp angle.

Enfiler une perle sur l'épingle et saisir avec l'outil 3 en 1 pour le travail des perles à l'endroit désiré pour la base de la boucle (nos motifs prévoient une longueur libre sur l'épingle). Plier la tige sur le bec de l'outil pour former un angle aigu.

Using 3-in-1 beading tool, grasp the wire at the bend, and wrap the short wire tail around the tool's jaw to form 3/4 of the loop.

À l'aide de l'outil 3 en 1 pour le travail des perles, saisir la tige au niveau du pli et enrouler la tige courte autour du bec pour former les 3/4 de la boucle.

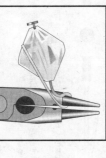

Readjust the tool slightly inside the loop to expose the unwrapped area, and complete the wrap of the loop.

Déplacer l'outil légèrement à l'intérieur de la boucle pour exposer une longueur encore droite, et continuer d'enrouler pour compléter la boucle.

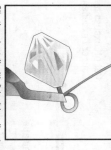

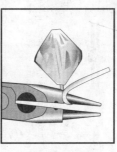

Clip the wire tail with 3-in-1 beading tool to finish.

Couper la queue de la tige à l'aide de l'outil 3 en 1 pour le travail des perles pour terminer.

TROUSSE
POUR LA
CONFECTION
DE BIJOUX

JEWELRY KIT

Super Style

Helpful Beading Tips
Conseils Utiles Pour le
Travail des Perles

Findings / Trouvailles

Tiger Tail • Queue de tigre

A widely used multi-purpose stringing material, very useful for heavier weight beads such as glass and stone. It consists of a number of strands of thin steel wire with a nylon coating. It is stiff so it does not require a needle and holds its shape.

Support à perler polyvalent couramment utilisé, trè utile pour les perles de verre et de pierre plus lourdes. Il est composé de plusieurs brins d'une tige d'acier trè fine recouverte d'une gaine de nylon. Il est rigide, alors il n'est pas nécessaire d'employer une aiguille pour l'enfiler, et il conserve sa forme.

Lobster Claw Clasp • Fermoirs pinces de homard

Lobster claw clasps are one of the most secure of clasps. They are best for jewelry strung with glass or stone or other heavy beads.

Les pinces de homard sont l'un des types de fermoirs les plus sûrs sur le marché. Ils conviennent parfaitement aux bijoux comportant des perles faites de verre, de pierre ou d'autres matières lourdes.

Head-Pin • Broche avec tête

Head pin

Crimp Beads • Perle d'arrêt

Crimp beads yield a secure and professional start and finish for beaded designs. They have an ultra-smooth finish and often come plated in colors. They protect and secure beading material and create nicely finished ends that do not need to be hidden. You can also use crimp spacers in jewelry designs.

Les perles d'arrêt permettent de commencer et de finir un bijou de perles de manière sûre et d'allure professionnelle. Le fini est ultra lisse et elles sont plaquées. Elles protègent et solidifient le fil et créent des extrémités dont la finition

Tools / Outils

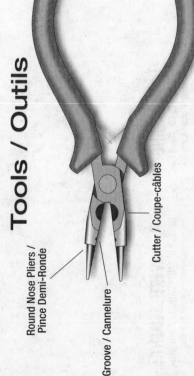

Round Nose Pliers /
Pince Demi-Ronde

Groove / Cannelure

Cutter / Coupe-câbles

Stringing beads / Enfiler les perles

This kit includes tiger tail for stringing, but you can use any kind of stringing material that fits through the bead holes.

De la queue de tigre est fournie avec cette trousse, mais il esr possible d'utiliser tout autre support à perler qui peut entrer dans les orifices des perles.

1. Cut your tiger tail 6" longer than your finished piece will be.
1. Couper la queue de tigre à 15 cm (6 po) de plus que la longueur totale du bijou.

2. Slip on a crimp bead at one end, and then slip on your clasp. Loop the end of your tiger tail back through the crimp bead leaving a 2" tail.
2. Glisser une perle d'arrêt à une extrémité, puis enfiler le fermoir. Faire repasser la queue de tigre dans la perle d'arrêt pour former une boucle, laissant une longueur de 5cm (2 po) dépassel.

Clasp / Fermoir

Crimp Bead / Perle d'arrêt

2'' tail / Excédent de 5 cm (2 po)

3. Use long-nose pliers to squeeze the crimp bead flat. It should not move if you have flattened it well.
3. Aplatir la perle d'arrêt à la pince à long bec. Le support ne devrait plus bouger si la perle a bien été aplatie.

4. Using other end of the tiger tail, string beads in your finished pattern. Help the first few beads over the 2" tail so it is hidden in the beads.
4. Enfiler les perles selon le motif conçu sur la planche dans l'autre extrémité de la queue de tigre. Enfiler également la longueur de 5 cm (2 po) qui dépasse dans les perles afin qu'elle soit cachée.

5. After you are done stringing, slip on another crimp bead and then the the other end of the clasp. As before, take the end of the tiger tial and loop it back through the crimp bead and under the last 2" of beads.
5. Une fois toutes les perles enfilées, glisser une autre perle d'arrêt et l'autre extrémité du fermoir sur le fil. Comme auparavant, faire repasser la queue de tigre dans la perle d'arrêt et dans la dernière section de perles de 5 cm (2 po).

Cut off excess tail
Couper l'excédent

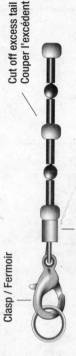

Flattened Crimp Bead / Perle d'arrêt aplatie

Clasp / Fermoir

6. Squeeze crimp bead flat and check for secure hold, then cut off extra tiger tail.
6. Aplatir la perle d'arrêt et vérifier la solidité de la fixation, puis couper le surplus de queue de tigre.

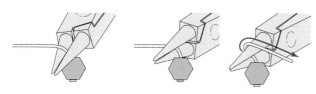

Thread a crystal on a head pin with a flat bottom. Grasp the pin with the pliers about $1/8"$ from the end of the jaws. The pliers should be touching the top of the crystal. Bend the wire at a 90° angle.

Pivot the pliers from horizontal to vertical.

Wrap the wire around the top jaw of the pliers

Reposition wire on the bottom jaw of the pliers. Wrap the wire around the bottom jaw of the pliers.

Grasp the loop of the dangle with the pliers. Without touching the crystal, begin coiling the short end around the neck of the dangle. Begin coils as close to the loop as possible. Make two or three coils, then clip the end of the wire close to the coils.

Repeat steps 1 - 5 for a total of 3 crystal and 5 pearl dangles.

Thread a leaf on a piece of wire and bend the wire.

Wrap the wire around the top jaw of the pliers.

Grasp the loop with the pliers. Without touching the leaf on the wire, begin coiling the long end around both wires. Begin coils as close to the loop as possible. Make 2 or 3 coils, then clip the end of the wire close to the coils.

Open the loop on the ear wire and thread on the leaf. Slip all 5 dangles on the ear wire loop alternating pearls and crystals. Close the ear wire loop.

Repeat all steps for the remaining earring.

Leaf Earrings

1 love leaves and you will too when you match them up with this cluster of peach crystals and pearl dangles.

designed by Jane Merchant

Materials:
6 peach 4mm Swarovski beads (A)
10 white 3mm x 4mm pearls (B)
16 sterling $1^1/2"$ flat head pins (F)
2 3' pieces of 24 gauge sterling wire (E)
2 aqua 18mm x 23mm carved stone leaves (D)
pair of sterling ear wires (C)
round-nose pliers

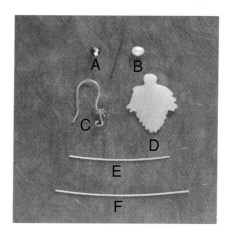

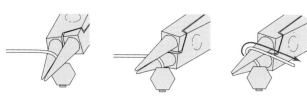

Separate crystals into two groups according to color.

Thread a crystal on a head pin with a flat bottom. Grasp pin with pliers about 1/8" from the end of the jaws. The pliers should be touching the top of the crystal. Bend the wire at a 90° angle .

Pivot the pliers from horizontal to vertical.

Wrap the wire around the top jaw of the pliers.

Reposition the wire on the bottom jaw of the pliers. Wrap wire around the bottom jaw of the pliers.

Grasp the loop of the dangle with the pliers. Without touching the crystal, begin coiling the short end around the neck of the dangle. Begin the coils as close to the loop as possible. Make 2 or 3 coils, then clip the end of the wire close to the coils.

Repeat steps 1 - 5 for a total of 5 crystal dangles.

Thread a chalcedony bead on a head pin with a ball bottom. Grasp the pin with the pliers about 1/8" from the end of the jaws. The pliers should be touching the top of the bead. Bend the wire at a 90° angle.

Clusters

Capture the feel of ice blue with the cool colors and crystalline sparkle of chalcedony beads and bicones. This is a creative way to use these large beads in something other than a pendant.

Materials:
10 crystal 4mm Swarovski bicones (A)
2 green 10mm x 16mm chalcedony beads (C)
10 sterling 1 1/2" flat head pins (D)
2 sterling 1 1/2" ball head pins (E)
pair of sterling ear wires (B)
round-nose pliers

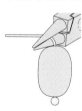  

Pivot the pliers from horizontal to vertical.

Wrap the wire around the top jaw of the pliers.

Reposition the wire on the bottom jaw of the pliers. Wrap the wire around the bottom jaw of the pliers.

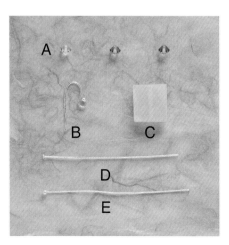

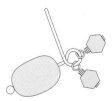 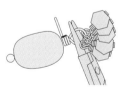 

Slip all 5 dangles on the loop.

Grasp the loop with the pliers. Without touching the bead on the head pin, begin coiling the short end around the neck. Begin the coils as close to the loop as possible.

Make 2 or 3 coils, then clip the end of the wire close to the coils.

Arrange the dangles as shown. Open the loop on the ear wire and thread on the earring. Close the ear wire loop.

Repeat all steps for the remaining earring.

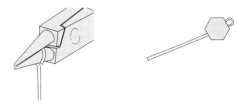

Turn a loop in one end of the wire with the pliers about 3/8" from the end of the jaw. Thread on a crystal.

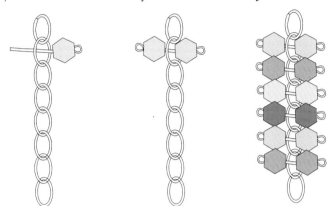

Pass straight end of wire through the second link of chain.

Thread on another crystal. Trim the end of wire to 3/8" and turn a loop.

Repeat steps 1 - 4 five more times to complete one chain, referring to photo for colors.

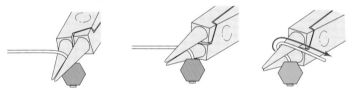

Thread a crystal on a head pin. Grasp the pin with pliers about 1/8" from the end of the jaws. The pliers should be touching the top of the bead. Bend the wire at a 90° angle .

Pivot the pliers from horizontal to vertical.

Wrap the wire around the top jaw of the pliers.

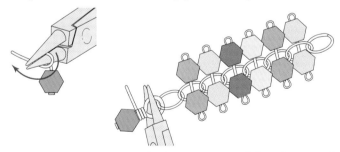

Reposition the wire on the bottom jaw of the pliers and wrap the wire around the bottom jaw of the pliers. Slip the wire loop onto last loop of chain.

Grasp the loop with the pliers and without touching the bead on the head pin, begin coiling the short end around the neck. Begin the coils as close to the loop as possible. Make 2 or 3 coils, then clip end of wire close to the coils.

Repeat to make 3 more drops. Open ear wire loop and thread crystal cluster on the earring.

Close the ear wire loop.

Repeat above steps for the remaining earring.

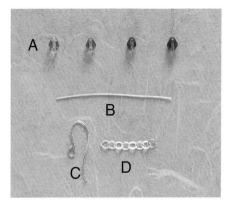

Crystal Cluster

The fiery brilliance of amber captures the eye as these earrings glitter in any light. Perfect for an elegant evening or a Saturday afternoon, wear these gorgeous crystals with jeans or your favorite dress.

Materials:
Swarovski 4mm crystals: 10 light green. 10 amber, 6 light amber, 6 brown (A)
12" of gold filled 24 gauge wire cut into 1" pieces (B)
two 2" pieces of gold filled chain with eight links each (D)
pair of gold filled ear wires (C)
eight head pins
round-nose pliers

Cut a 4" long piece of 22 gauge wire. Grasp the wire with round-nose pliers about 1¹/₄" from the top. Bend the wire at a 90° angle.

Let your grip loosen on the pliers and pivot them from horizontal to vertical.

Wrap the short piece of wire over the top jaw of pliers.

  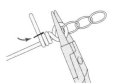

Reposition the wire on the bottom jaw of the pliers. Complete the loop by wrapping the short end of the wire around the bottom jaw of the pliers.

Thread the last link of a piece of chain on the loop as shown.

Without touching the long end of the wire, begin coiling the shorter piece of wire around the longer piece. Begin coils as close to the loop as possible. Make 2 or 3 coils then clip the end of wire close to the coils.

Thread the cone and a potato pearl on the long end of the wire. Grasp the wire with the pliers about ¹/₈" from the end of the jaws. The pliers should be touching the top of the pearl. Bend the wire at a 90° angle.

Pivot the pliers from horizontal to vertical.

Wrap the wire around the top jaw of the pliers.

Move the piece to the bottom jaw of the pliers and complete the loop.

Begin coiling the wire around the neck of the earring. Begin coils as close to the loop as possible. Make 2 or 3 coils then clip the end of wire close to the coils.

Thread a flat pearl on a head pin. Make a loop with the head pin just as you did for the top of the earring.

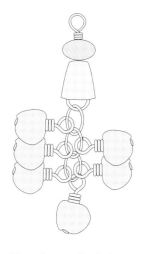

Slip the end of the pin through the first link in the chain. Wrap the loop with 2 or 3 coils. Clip the end of wire close to coils.

Repeat with 5 more flat pearls. Refer to illustration for placement.

Slip the top loop of the earring on the earring wire.

Repeat all steps for the other earring.

Pearl Clusters

Since their discovery, pearls have been revered as one of the world's most beautiful gems. Legend names these gifts of nature "dewdrops filled with moonlight". These cluster earrings certainly live up to the legend.

Materials:
12 keishi 10mm disk pearls (B)
12 sterling 2" head pins (E)
2 hill tribe 3mm x 4mm silver cones (C)
2 potato 8mm pearls
2 sterling 1/4" pieces of chain
pair of sterling ear wires (D)
8" of 22 gauge sterling wire
round-nose pliers

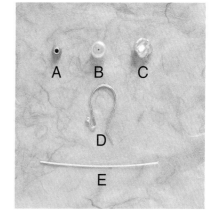

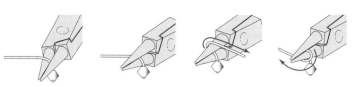

Thread a bicone crystal on a head pin. Grasp the pin with pliers about 1/8" from the end of the jaws. The pliers should be touching the top of the crystal. Bend the wire at a 90° angle.

Pivot the pliers from horizontal to vertical.

Wrap the wire around the top jaw of the pliers.

Reposition the wire on the bottom jaw of the pliers. Wrap the wire around the bottom jaw of the pliers.

Slip straight end of a head pin through the bottom link of one piece of chain. Grasp loop of dangle with the pliers.

Without touching the disk bead begin coiling the short end around the neck of the dangle. Begin the coils as close to the loop as possible. Make 2 or 3 coils, then clip the end of the wire close to the coils.

Thread a teardrop with a 4" piece of 24 gauge silver wire. Arrange wire with one side shorter than the other. Cross wire ends. Then bend ends at a 90 degree angle. Grasp longer wire with pliers about 1/8" from the end of the jaws. Bend the wire at a 90° angle.

Pivot pliers from horizontal to vertical. Wrap the wire around the top jaw of pliers.

Reposition wire on the bottom jaw of pliers. Wrap the wire around the bottom jaw of the pliers.

Thread on one end link of the chain. Grasp the loop with the pliers. Begin coiling one end around both wires. Begin coils as close to the loop as possible. Make 2 or 3 coils, then clip the end of the coiling wire and the straight wire close to the coils.

Onyx & Stick Pearls

Totally elegant, and as unique as the wearer, this combination of onyx and stick pearls will have everyone asking what designer made your custom earrings.

Materials:
stick pearls: two 10mm, two 10mm and two 20mm (E)
two 10mm onyx disks (D)
six 5mm x 5mm faceted black glass teardrops (C)
six 4mm crystal AB Swarovski bicones (A)
6mm Bali silver bead cap (B)
pieces of sterling silver chain with 3mm x 4mm links:
    six 1/2", six 3/4" (G)
six 1 1/2" sterling silver head pins with ball ends (I)
eight 4" pieces of sterling silver wire (H)
pair of sterling silver ear wires (F)
round-nose pliers
wire cutters

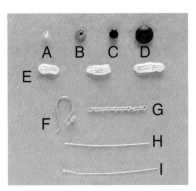

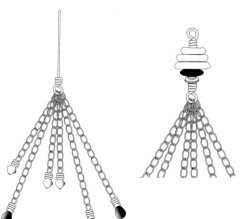

Make a wrapped loop on one end of a longer piece of wire and attach chains.

Slip bead cap, onyx disk and 3 pearls on wire. Make a wrapped loop at other end of wire.

Open ear wire loop, thread loop on the earring and close the ear wire loop.

Repeat above steps for the remaining earring.

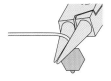 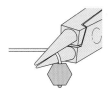

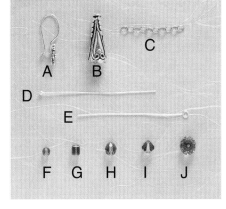

Thread nailhead crystal on a head pin . Grasp the pin with pliers about 1/8" from the end of the jaws. Pliers should be touching the top of the crystal. Bend the wire at a 90° angle.

Pivot pliers from horizontal to vertical.

Wrap the wire around the top jaw of the pliers.

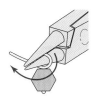

Reposition wire on the bottom jaw of the pliers. Wrap the wire around the bottom jaw of the pliers.

Slip dangle on 2" chain.

Grasp the loop of the dangle with pliers. Without touching the crystal, begin coiling the end of the wire around the neck of the dangle. Begin coils as close to the loop as possible. Make 2 or 3 coils, then clip the end of the wire close to the coils.

Cone Chain Dangles

Amethyst crystals cascade from silver cones in a waterfall of sparkle. Make delicious dangles with this simple technique.

Materials:
amethyst Swarovski crystals:
two 4mm bicones
four 4mm round (F)
two 4mm cubes (G)
two 6mm bicones (I)
two 6mm round (H)
two 8mm nailhead (J)
two 8mm x 20mm Bali silver cones (B)
two 3" sterling silver eye pins (E)
11 pieces of sterling silver chain with 3mm x 4mm links
    in graduated lengths of 1" to 2" (C)
twenty-two 1¹/₂" sterling silver head pins with ball ends (D)
pair of sterling silver ear wires (A)
round-nose pliers

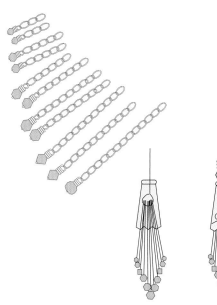

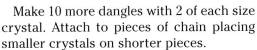

Make 10 more dangles with 2 of each size crystal. Attach to pieces of chain placing smaller crystals on shorter pieces.

Slip all pieces of chain on eye pin and pull into the cone.

Slip a 4mm round crystal and the ear wire loop onto the eye pin and repeat steps 1 through 6 to make a wrapped loop.

Repeat all steps for the remaining earring.

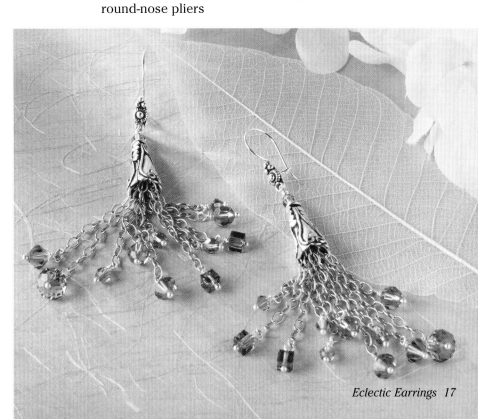

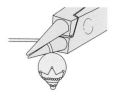

Thread a bead cap and a coin pearl on a head pin. Grasp the pin with pliers about 1/8" from the end of the jaws.

The pliers should be touching the top of the coin pearl. Bend the wire at a 90˚ angle .

Pivot pliers from horizontal to vertical.

Wrap the wire around the top jaw of pliers.

Reposition the wire on the bottom jaw of the pliers. Wrap the wire around the bottom jaw of the pliers.

Slip the straight end of the head pin through the bottom link of the 1" chain and grasp the loop of the dangle with the pliers.

Without touching the pearl, begin coiling the short end around the neck of the dangle. Begin coils as close to the loop as possible.

Make 2 or 3 coils, then clip the end of the wire close to the coils.

Pearl Goddess

Pearls accentuate a woman's natural beauty. These delicate gold strands show off the popular goddess charm while small clusters of pearls shimmer with natural luster.

designed by Jane Merchant

Materials:
two 1/2" gold color pewter goddesses (J)
pearls: two 10mm disks (B), four 6mm x 8mm (A))
two 6mm gold stardust beads (D)
two gold 6mm bead caps (E)
pieces of gold filled chain with 3mm x 4mm links:
    two 1 1/2", two 1", two 1/2" (H)
eight 2" gold filled head pins with ball ends (G)
gold filled figure 8 ring (F)
two 5mm gold filled split rings (C)
pair of gold filled ear wires (I)
round-nose pliers

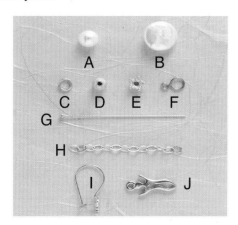

Make dangles with remaining pearls and stardust beads and attach them to the 1" chain.

Use a split ring to connect the goddess charm to the bottom loop of the longest chain.

Thread a 1 1/2", 1" and 1/2" chain on the large end of a figure 8 ring. Open ear wire loop and thread on the small end of the figure 8 ring. Close the ear wire loop.

Repeat above steps for the remaining earring.